North Palm Beach Public Library
303 Anchorage Drive
North Palm Beach, FL   33408

PYTHONS

DOUG WECHSLER

ACADEMY OF NATURAL SCIENCES

The Rosen Publishing Group's
PowerKids Press™
New York

For Uncle Sonny, who has a python-sized heart

About the Author
Wildlife biologist, ornithologist, and photographer Doug Wechsler has studied birds, snakes, frogs, and other wildlife
around the world. Doug Wechsler works at The Academy of Natural Sciences of Philadelphia, a natural history
museum. As part of his job, he travels to rain forests and remote parts of the world to take pictures of birds. He has
taken part in expeditions to Ecuador, the Philippines, Borneo, Cuba, Cameroon, and many other countries.

Published in 2001 by The Rosen Publishing Group, Inc.
29 East 21st Street, New York, NY 10010

First Edition

Book Design: Michael de Guzman

Photo Credits: pp. 4, 7, 12, 15, 16, 20 © Doug Wechsler; p. 8 © Anthony Bannister; Gallo Images/CORBIS; p. 11 © David
A. Northcott/CORBIS; p. 19 © Joe McDonald/CORBIS; p. 20 © Chris Mattison; Frank Lane Picture Agency/CORBIS; p. 22 ©
Robert Pickett/CORBIS.

Wechsler, Doug.
    Pythons / Wechsler, Doug.—1st ed.
      p. cm.— (The really wild life of snakes)
    Summary: Briefly describes the physical characteristics, behavior, and habitat of pythons, along with some interesting facts
about these snakes.
    ISBN 0-8239-5604-0 (alk. paper)
  1. Pythons—Juvenile literature. [1. Pythons. 2. Snakes.] I. Title.

QL666.O63 W43 2000
597.96'78—dc21   00-023747

Manufactured in the United States of America

CONTENTS

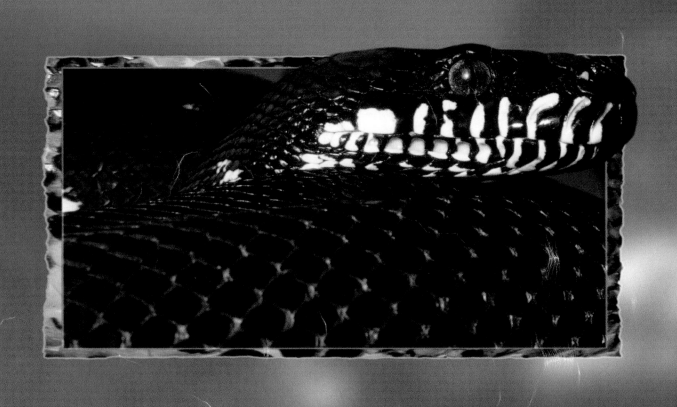

CHAMPION SNAKES

What is the only snake known to have eaten a person? What snake has eaten the biggest meal? If you answered "python" to each of these questions, you are right. Pythons hold many records. Pythons are a group of **stout**, or thick-bodied, snakes. They live in Africa, Asia, and Australia. Only five kinds of snakes in the world grow more than 20 feet (6.1 m) long. Four of these are pythons. Most types of pythons do not grow bigger than eight feet (2.4 m) long. The dwarf python rarely gets bigger than two feet (0.6 m) long. Pythons are related to boas and look a lot like them. Pythons and boas are **constrictors**. They kill their **prey** by squeezing it to death.

This type of python, called Boelen's python, lives only in the mountains on the island of New Guinea. There are about 26 species of pythons.

WHERE TO FIND A PYTHON

Pythons live in the **tropics**. Some, like the **reticulated** python and the green tree python, live in rain forests. Reticulated pythons crawl on the forest floor and swim in nearby water. Green tree pythons live high in the branches of forest trees. They are well **camouflaged** among the green leaves. African rock pythons live in bushy areas, grasslands, and forests. The adults like to be in or near water. The young rock pythons often live in rocky areas. Perhaps that is how they got their name. The woma is a python that is active at night in the deserts of Australia.

The green tree python lives in the trees of the rain forest. Its green skin allows it to hide easily among the green leaves.